The Art and Science of AI Prompt Engineering

Crafting Instructions for Intelligent Machines

Detailed Book Introduction :

Welcome to the fascinating world of AI prompt engineering, a field where human creativity and machine intelligence converge. In an era where artificial intelligence (AI) is transforming industries and redefining possibilities, the ability to communicate effectively with AI systems has become a critical skill. This book is your guide to mastering that skill.

AI prompt engineering is more than just asking questions or giving commands; it's about crafting instructions that elicit the most relevant, accurate, and insightful responses from AI models. Whether you're a developer, researcher, marketer, writer, or simply curious about AI, understanding prompt engineering will empower you to harness the full potential of AI tools like ChatGPT, GPT-4, and other language models.

In this book, we'll delve into the theory and practice of prompt engineering, exploring the underlying principles and providing practical techniques for interacting with different types of AI models. We'll cover everything from the basics of prompt design to advanced strategies for fine-tuning prompts and optimizing results.

You'll learn:

- **The Fundamentals:** What AI prompts are, how they work, and why they matter.
- **The Art of Crafting Prompts:** Techniques for writing clear, concise, and effective prompts for various tasks like writing, research, code generation, and more.
- **The Science of Prompt Engineering:** How to evaluate prompt performance, experiment with different approaches, and iterate for continuous improvement.
- **Advanced Techniques:** Strategies for handling complex prompts, incorporating context, and addressing bias in AI responses.

- **Real-World Applications:** How prompt engineering is used in diverse fields, from content creation and customer service to scientific research and software development.

Throughout the book, we'll share real-world examples, case studies, and practical exercises to help you apply the concepts you learn. We'll also discuss the ethical considerations of AI prompt engineering and how to use this powerful tool responsibly.

Whether you're a beginner or an experienced AI practitioner, this book will equip you with the knowledge and skills you need to become a proficient prompt engineer and unlock the full potential of AI.

Table of Contents:

Chapter 1

Introduction to AI Prompt Engineering

Welcome to the fascinating world of AI prompt engineering, where the art of human communication meets the power of artificial intelligence. This chapter lays the groundwork for your journey as a prompt engineer, introducing you to this rapidly evolving field's fundamental concepts, terminology, and significance.

Defining Prompt Engineering:

At its core, prompt engineering is the process of designing and crafting effective instructions, or *prompts*, to guide the output of AI models. These prompts act as a bridge between human intention and machine understanding, enabling us to communicate our goals and expectations to AI systems in a way they can comprehend and act upon.

Think of it like giving directions to a helpful but literal-minded assistant. If you want a delicious meal, you wouldn't just say "make me food." Instead, you'd provide specific instructions: "Prepare a vegetarian pasta dish with garlic, spinach, and sun-dried tomatoes." In prompt engineering, we're crafting similarly detailed instructions for AI models.

Why Prompt Engineering Matters:

In the era of AI-powered tools and applications, prompt engineering has become an essential skill. Here's why:

1. **Unlocking AI's Potential:** AI models, while powerful, are only as good as the instructions they receive. Effective prompts act as a key to unlocking the full potential of AI. For example, a well-crafted prompt can transform a language

model from a simple chatbot into a creative writing partner, a research assistant, or a coding collaborator.

2. **Improving Human-AI Interaction:** Prompt engineering bridges the communication gap between humans and machines. By crafting clear and concise prompts, we can ensure that AI understands our intent and delivers the desired results. This leads to more productive and satisfying interactions, whether we're using AI for work, learning, or creative pursuits.

3. **Driving Innovation:** Prompt engineering is a catalyst for innovation. By experimenting with different prompts, we can explore new ways to leverage AI's capabilities and discover novel applications that were previously unimaginable. For instance, prompt engineering has led to breakthroughs in AI-assisted drug discovery, creative content generation, and even climate modeling.

The Building Blocks of Prompt Engineering:

1. **Prompts:** A prompt is the input you provide to an AI model. It can be a question, an instruction, or even a partial sentence. The prompt sets the stage for the AI's response and determines the direction it takes.

   *Example: "Explain the concept of quantum entanglement in simple terms."

2. **AI Models:** These are sophisticated algorithms trained on massive datasets to perform various tasks. Large language models (LLMs) like GPT-3 and ChatGPT excel at understanding and generating human-like text.

3. **Output:** This is the AI model's response to your prompt. The quality of the output depends on the clarity, specificity, and relevance of your prompt, as well as the capabilities of the AI model itself.

Types of Prompts (with Examples):

- **Instruction-Based:** "Write a product description for a new smartphone, highlighting its camera features."
- **Question-Based:** "What are the potential risks associated with gene editing technology?"
- **Completion-Based:** "Albert Einstein's most famous equation is E=..."

The Prompt Engineering Process:

1. **Define the Goal:** Determine what you want to achieve with the AI model. What kind of information, output, or action are you seeking?
2. **Craft the Prompt:** Design a clear and concise prompt that accurately conveys your goal and provides enough context for the AI model to understand.
3. **Evaluate the Output:** Assess the AI's response. Is it relevant, accurate, and helpful? Does it meet your expectations?
4. **Iterate and Refine:** If the output is not satisfactory, revise your prompt and try again. Experiment with different phrasing, add more context, or try a different AI model.

The Importance of Context (with Example):

Imagine asking an AI to "write a summary." Without context, the AI wouldn't know what to summarize. However, providing context like "Summarize the key findings of the latest

IPCC report on climate change" gives the AI the necessary information to generate a meaningful and relevant response.

Beyond the Basics:

As you progress through this book, you'll discover more advanced prompt engineering techniques that will empower you to harness the full potential of AI.

Chapter 2

Understanding AI Models

The Engine Room of Effective Prompts

In the world of AI, a "model" is the heart and brain of any AI system. It's a complex algorithm trained on vast amounts of data to recognize patterns, understand language, and generate responses. This chapter will delve into the inner workings of these models, focusing on the types most commonly used in prompt engineering. By understanding how AI models function, you'll be better equipped to craft prompts that elicit the responses you desire.

Types of AI Models for Prompt Engineering:

1. **Large Language Models (LLMs):**
- **What they are:** LLMs are a type of artificial intelligence model that are trained on a massive dataset of text and code. They can generate text, translate languages, write different kinds of creative content, and answer your questions in an informative way.
- **How they work:** LLMs use a transformer architecture, which allows them to process information in parallel. They also use a technique called attention to focus on the most important parts of the input.
- **Examples:** Some popular LLMs include GPT-3, GPT-4, LaMDA, and BLOOM.
- **Strengths:** LLMs are incredibly versatile and can be used for a wide range of tasks, including content creation, translation, and customer service.
- **Weaknesses:** LLMs can sometimes generate incorrect or nonsensical information, and they can be sensitive to the way a prompt is worded.
- **Use case examples:**

- ○ **Prompt:** "Write a poem about the beauty of a sunset."
- ○ **Output:** "The sun descends, a fiery ball, / Painting the sky with hues surreal. / Clouds ablaze, a vibrant wall, / Reflecting in the ocean's appeal."
- ○ **Prompt:** "Summarize the key points from this article about climate change." (with the article provided)
- ○ **Output:** (A concise summary of the article's key points)

2. **Text-to-Image Models:**

- **What they are:** These models generate images based on textual descriptions or prompts.
- **How they work:** Text-to-image models use a combination of natural language processing and computer vision techniques to understand the text input and generate corresponding images.
- **Examples:** Some popular text-to-image models include DALL-E 2, Stable Diffusion, and Midjourney.
- **Strengths:** Text-to-image models can create unique and imaginative visuals, opening up new possibilities for creative expression and design.
- **Weaknesses:** The quality of the output can vary depending on the complexity of the prompt and the capabilities of the model.
- **Use case examples:**
  - ○ **Prompt:** "A watercolor painting of a cat sitting in a sunbeam."
  - ○ **Output:** (An image matching the description)
  - ○ **Prompt:** "A photorealistic image of a futuristic city with flying cars."
  - ○ **Output:** (An image matching the description)

3. **Code Generation Models:**

- **What they are:** These models generate code snippets or even entire programs based on natural language descriptions of the desired functionality.

- **How they work:** Code generation models are typically trained on large datasets of code and use similar techniques to LLMs to understand and generate code.
- **Examples:** OpenAI Codex, GitHub Copilot
- **Strengths:** Code generation models can automate repetitive coding tasks, accelerate development, and help non-programmers create simple applications.
- **Weaknesses:** Generated code may not always be perfect and might require human review and correction.
- **Use case examples:**
  - **Prompt:** "Write a Python function to sort a list of numbers in ascending order."
  - **Output:** (A Python code snippet that performs the sorting task)
  - **Prompt:** "Create a basic HTML structure for a website with a header, navigation bar, main content area, and footer."
  - **Output:** (HTML code for the described website structure)

Understanding Model Limitations:

While AI models are incredibly powerful, they have limitations. Being aware of these limitations is crucial for effective prompt engineering:

- **Hallucination:** AI models can sometimes generate incorrect or nonsensical information, especially when dealing with ambiguous or incomplete prompts.
- **Bias:** Models may inadvertently perpetuate biases present in their training data, leading to skewed or discriminatory outputs.
- **Sensitivity to Wording:** Slight changes in wording can sometimes drastically alter the model's response.
- **Limited Contextual Understanding:** While models like LLMs are designed to understand context, they might struggle with nuanced or complex contexts.

Choosing the Right Model:

Selecting the appropriate AI model is crucial for achieving your desired outcome. Consider the following factors:

- **Task:** What do you want the AI to do? Choose a model that specializes in that specific task.
- **Complexity:** How complex is your prompt? Some models are better at handling more complex instructions than others.
- **Desired Output:** What kind of output are you looking for? Choose a model that can generate the type of output you need.
- **Resources:** Consider the computational resources you have available. Some models are more computationally intensive than others.

By understanding the different types of AI models and their limitations, you can make informed decisions about which model to use and how to craft prompts that maximize its potential. This knowledge is the foundation for effective prompt engineering and will empower you to harness the power of AI for a wide range of applications.

Sources

info

1. www.nptechforgood.com/2023/04/23/how-to-enhance-your-nonprofits-written-content-with-artificial-intelligence/

Chapter 3

Crafting Prompts

The Essentials

You now understand the inner workings of AI models and the pivotal role they play in prompt engineering. Let's transform that knowledge into practical skills by exploring the core elements of crafting effective prompts. Think of prompts as the steering wheel for AI models, guiding them toward the desired destination of your output. This chapter equips you with the tools to navigate that journey.

The Anatomy of a High-Quality Prompt:

1. **Clarity and Specificity:**

- **Clear Language:** Use precise and unambiguous language to avoid confusion. Avoid vague phrases and jargon that the AI model might not understand.

- **Specific Instructions:** Clearly state the task you want the model to perform. Use action verbs like "summarize," "analyze," "compare," "generate," or "translate."

Example:

- **Vague Prompt:** "Tell me about dogs."
- **Specific Prompt:** "Describe the physical characteristics, temperament, and common uses of the Labrador Retriever dog breed."
2. **Context and Background Information:**
- **Setting the Stage:** Provide the AI model with the necessary background information to understand your request fully. This could include relevant facts,

details about the topic, or even the intended audience for the output.

- **Guiding the Response:** Context can help steer the AI model towards a more relevant and accurate response.

Example:

- **Prompt (Lacking Context):** "Write a poem about love."
- **Prompt (With Context):** "Write a sonnet about the unrequited love of a young poet for their muse, using vivid imagery and metaphors to convey the depth of their emotions."

3. **Instructions:**

- **Action Verbs:** Use strong verbs to clearly state the task you want the model to perform.
- **Desired Format:** Specify the format of the output you expect, such as a bullet-point list, essay, poem, or code snippet.
- **Length:** If applicable, define the desired length of the response.

Example:

- **Prompt:** "Generate a list of five creative marketing slogans for a new electric car, each slogan should be catchy and emphasize sustainability."

4. **Constraints:**

- **Limiting the Scope:** Constraints help to focus the AI model's response by setting boundaries on the content, style, or tone.
- **Avoiding Overwhelm:** Constraints prevent the model from generating overly broad or unfocused responses.

Example:

- **Prompt:** "Write a 500-word persuasive essay arguing for the adoption of renewable energy sources. The essay should be aimed at a general audience and avoid technical jargon."

5. **Examples (Optional):**

- **Illustrating the Desired Output:** Providing examples of similar outputs can be helpful, especially for creative or complex tasks.
- **Guiding the Model's Style:** Examples can also help to guide the model's writing style or tone.

Example:

- **Prompt:** "Write a product description for a new smartwatch in the style of Apple's marketing copy."
- **Example:** (Provide a sample of Apple's marketing copy for reference)

Real-World Examples of Effective Prompts:

- **Summarization:** "Summarize the key findings of this scientific article on the effects of caffeine on cognitive function: [article link]."

- **Analysis:** "Analyze the economic impact of remote work on urban areas, considering factors like real estate prices, transportation, and local businesses."

- **Comparison:** "Compare and contrast the philosophies of Stoicism and Epicureanism, highlighting their key differences in ethics, happiness, and the meaning of life."

- **Generation:** "Write a short story about a young musician who discovers a magical instrument that grants wishes."

- **Translation:** "Translate this news article from English to Spanish while preserving the original meaning and tone: [article link]."

By incorporating these essential elements and best practices into your prompt crafting, you'll be well on your way to harnessing the full potential of AI models for a wide range of applications. Remember, prompt engineering is an iterative process. Don't be afraid to experiment, refine your prompts based on feedback, and continue learning to elevate your skills.

Chapter 4

Prompt Engineering for Writing and Content Creation

The synergy between artificial intelligence and human creativity is revolutionizing how we write and create content. AI isn't just a tool for data analysis; it's a versatile writing assistant that can spark ideas, refine drafts, and even help you overcome writer's block. In this chapter, we'll delve into the exciting possibilities of using prompt engineering to elevate your writing process and unleash your creative potential.

AI as Your Collaborative Writing Partner:

Think of AI as your collaborator, an ever-available brainstorming partner, editor, and muse. It can help you generate a wealth of ideas, provide diverse perspectives, and polish your writing to perfection. The key is to master the art of crafting prompts that effectively guide the AI towards the results you desire.

Example: Brainstorming Blog Post Ideas

- **Prompt:** "I'm a lifestyle blogger interested in sustainable living. Generate 10 blog post ideas focusing on eco-friendly travel tips."

- **AI Response:**

    1. Top 10 Eco-Friendly Destinations for Conscious Travelers
    2. How to Pack Light and Reduce Your Carbon Footprint on Your Next Trip
    3. Sustainable Travel Hacks: Eco-Conscious Choices on a Budget
    4. Exploring Local Cuisine: A Guide to Eating Sustainably While Traveling
    5. Off-the-Beaten-Path: Eco-Tourism Destinations That Support Local Communities

6. Carbon Offsetting: How to Make Your Travels More Sustainable

7. Sustainable Transportation Options: Trains, Buses, and Bikes for Green Globetrotters

8. Eco-Friendly Accommodations: Choosing Hotels and Hostels That Prioritize Sustainability

9. Volunteering While Traveling: Giving Back to the Communities You Visit

10. Sustainable Souvenirs: Ethical Shopping Tips for Mindful Travelers

•

Example: Outlining an Essay

- **Prompt:** "Create an outline for a persuasive essay arguing for the implementation of a four-day workweek, highlighting its benefits for employees, employers, and the environment."

- **AI Response:**

I. Introduction A. Hook: Present a startling statistic about employee burnout or the environmental impact of commuting. B. Thesis Statement: Argue that a four-day workweek is a viable solution that benefits employees, employers, and the environment.

II. Benefits for Employees A. Improved Work-Life Balance B. Reduced Stress and Burnout C. Increased Productivity and Focus D. Enhanced Mental and Physical Health

III. Benefits for Employers A. Higher Employee Retention Rates B. Increased Attraction of Top Talent C. Improved Employee Morale and Engagement D. Potential Cost Savings (Reduced Office Space, Utilities)

IV. Environmental Benefits A. Reduced Carbon Emissions from Commuting B. Decreased Energy Consumption in Offices C. Potential for Increased Recycling and Sustainable Practices

V. Addressing Potential Challenges A. Concerns About Productivity Loss (Provide counterarguments and evidence) B. Industry-Specific Implementation Issues (Offer solutions and examples)

VI. Conclusion A. Restate the thesis and summarize key points. B. Call to action: Urge readers to advocate for a four-day workweek in their workplaces or communities.

Example: Drafting and Editing Content

- **Prompt (Drafting):** "Draft a compelling introduction for a blog post about the benefits of meditation for stress reduction."

- **AI Response:** In today's fast-paced world, stress has become an unwelcome companion for many. But what if there was a simple yet powerful tool that could help you find inner peace and tranquility amidst the chaos? Enter meditation, a practice that has been scientifically proven to reduce stress, improve mental clarity, and enhance overall well-being.

- **Prompt (Editing):** "Rewrite the following sentence to make it more concise and impactful: 'The results of the study indicated a significant decrease in anxiety levels among participants who practiced mindfulness meditation regularly.'"

- **AI Response:** "Mindfulness meditation significantly reduced anxiety levels in study participants."

Example: Creative Writing

- **Prompt:** "Write a short story about a robot who discovers the meaning of friendship."
- **AI Response:** (The AI would generate a complete short story based on the prompt.)

Important Considerations:

- **Fact-Checking:** Always verify the accuracy of information generated by AI, especially for non-fiction writing.
- **Style and Tone:** Be explicit about the desired style and tone in your prompts to ensure the AI's output aligns with your vision.
- **Human Touch:** AI is a tool, not a replacement for human creativity. Use it to enhance your writing, not replace your unique voice and perspective.

By mastering the art of prompt engineering for writing and content creation, you can unlock new levels of creativity, productivity, and impact. Embrace AI as your collaborative partner and watch your writing soar to new heights.

Chapter 5

Prompt Engineering for Research and Information Gathering

The information age has ushered in an era of unprecedented access to knowledge. However, navigating the vast sea of data and extracting meaningful insights can be a daunting task. This is where AI, coupled with effective prompt engineering, emerges as a powerful ally for researchers, students, analysts, and anyone seeking to uncover valuable information.

AI: Your Research Navigator and Knowledge Synthesizer:

Think of AI as your research assistant, a tireless companion capable of sifting through mountains of data, pinpointing relevant sources, summarizing complex information, and even synthesizing knowledge from diverse perspectives. The key to harnessing this power lies in mastering the art of crafting prompts that guide AI models toward your research objectives.

Key Research Tasks AI Can Enhance:

1. **Information Retrieval:**
- **Finding Relevant Sources:** AI can be a powerful search engine, capable of identifying specific types of information across a wide range of sources.

   - **Example Prompt:** "Find me the latest peer-reviewed research articles on the impact of social media on adolescent mental health."
   - **AI Response:** A list of relevant articles from reputable journals like the *Journal of Adolescent Health* or *Cyberpsychology, Behavior, and Social Networking.*

- **Extracting Specific Information:** Once you have a relevant source, AI can pinpoint the exact details you need.

  - **Example Prompt:** "Summarize the key findings of this article on the relationship between sleep and memory consolidation."
  - **AI Response:** A concise summary of the study's findings, highlighting the link between sleep duration and memory performance.

2. **Synthesis and Analysis:**

- **Summarizing Information:** When dealing with lengthy reports, articles, or books, AI can condense the core information into a digestible format.

  - **Example Prompt:** "Summarize the main arguments presented in this government report on climate change mitigation strategies."
  - **AI Response:** A bulleted list or paragraph summarizing the report's key recommendations for reducing carbon emissions and adapting to climate change.

- **Comparing and Contrasting:** AI can analyze multiple sources and identify similarities and differences in their viewpoints, arguments, or data.

  - **Example Prompt:** "Compare and contrast the economic policies of two political candidates based on their public statements and campaign platforms."
  - **AI Response:** A table or structured text comparing the candidates' stances on taxation, healthcare, infrastructure, and other key economic issues.

3. **Generating Reports and Presentations:**

- **Creating Outlines:** AI can help structure your research findings into a coherent outline for a paper, presentation, or report.

  - **Example Prompt:** "Create an outline for a research paper on the potential benefits and risks of artificial intelligence in the workplace."
  - **AI Response:** A structured outline with sections on potential benefits (increased productivity, automation of repetitive tasks), potential risks (job displacement, bias in decision-making), and mitigation strategies.

- **Drafting Content:** AI can generate drafts for specific sections or even entire documents, providing a starting point for your own writing.

  - **Example Prompt:** "Write an introduction for a research paper on the historical development of artificial intelligence, highlighting key milestones and influential figures."
  - **AI Response:** An introductory paragraph that sets the stage for the research paper, mentioning pioneers like Alan Turing and key developments such as the invention of the perceptron.

Enhancing Your Research Process with Prompt Engineering:

- **Specificity:** The more precise your prompt, the more targeted and relevant the AI's response will be. Clearly define your research question or objective.

- **Contextual Clues:** Provide relevant background information to help the AI understand the context of your query. This might include the specific field of research, the time period, or any relevant terminology.

- **Iterative Refinement:** Don't be afraid to experiment with different prompts and refine them based on the AI's responses. Ask follow-up questions or provide additional context to guide the AI towards the information you seek.

- **Critical Evaluation:** Always critically evaluate the information provided by AI. Verify facts with reliable sources, consider potential biases in the AI model, and use your own judgment to interpret the findings.

Ethical Considerations in AI-Assisted Research:

- **Plagiarism:** While AI can generate content, it's important to avoid plagiarism by properly citing any information or ideas obtained from AI-generated text.

- **Bias:** Be aware of potential biases in AI models and critically evaluate the information they provide. Look for diverse perspectives and sources to ensure a balanced understanding of the topic.

By mastering prompt engineering for research, you can transform AI into a powerful ally that empowers you to explore vast amounts of information, uncover hidden insights, and ultimately, advance our collective knowledge and understanding of the world around us.

Chapter 6

Prompt Engineering for Code Generation and Programming

The landscape of software development is undergoing a transformation, and at the heart of this revolution is artificial intelligence. AI is no longer just a tool for data scientists; it's becoming an indispensable companion for programmers, capable of generating code snippets, automating repetitive tasks, and even explaining complex code concepts. This chapter will delve into how prompt engineering can be your key to unlocking the full potential of AI for your coding endeavors.

AI: Your Coding Co-Pilot:

Imagine having a coding partner who can instantly generate code snippets, refactor existing code, identify errors, and even explain the intricacies of complex algorithms. That's the potential of AI when guided by effective prompts. Whether you're a seasoned developer or just starting, AI can streamline your workflow, boost your productivity, and open up new possibilities for innovation.

Key Programming Tasks Enhanced by AI:

1. **Code Generation:**
- **Simple Snippets:** AI models can generate concise code snippets for common tasks, saving you precious time and effort.
    - **Example Prompt:** "Write a Python function to check if a number is prime."
    - **AI Response:**
- Python

```
def is_prime(num):

    if num <= 1:
```

```python
        return False

    for i in range(2, int(num**0.5) + 1):

        if num % i == 0:

            return False

    return True
```

-
- **Complex Functionality:** With the right prompts, AI can generate more intricate code structures, algorithms, or even complete functions.

    - **Example Prompt:** "Implement a recursive function in JavaScript to calculate the nth Fibonacci number."
    - **AI Response:**
- JavaScript

```javascript
function fibonacci(n) {

    if (n <= 1) return n;

    return fibonacci(n - 1) + fibonacci(n - 2);

}
```

-
-

2. **Code Explanation and Refactoring:**
- **Understanding Code:** AI can provide clear and concise explanations for unfamiliar code snippets, helping you learn and troubleshoot.

- ○ **Example Prompt:** "Explain how this Python decorator works: [insert code snippet]."
- ○ **AI Response:** A detailed explanation of the decorator's purpose, how it modifies the behavior of the function it decorates, and potential use cases.

- **Improving Code:** AI can suggest ways to refactor your code to make it more readable, efficient, or maintainable.

  - ○ **Example Prompt:** "Refactor this Java code to follow best practices and improve performance: [insert code snippet]."
  - ○ **AI Response:** A revised version of the code with suggestions for better variable naming, loop optimization, or more efficient data structures.

3. **Debugging and Error Handling:**
- **Identifying Errors:** AI can help pinpoint errors in your code, saving you time and frustration.

  - ○ **Example Prompt:** "Why am I getting a 'NullPointerException' in this Java code: [insert code snippet]?"
  - ○ **AI Response:** An explanation of what a NullPointerException is, why it's occurring in your code, and potential ways to fix it.

- **Suggesting Fixes:** AI can propose solutions to fix errors or improve your code's error handling mechanisms.

  - ○ **Example Prompt:** "Suggest a more robust error handling strategy for this Python API call: [insert code snippet]."

- **AI Response:** A revised code snippet that includes error checking, exception handling, and appropriate logging.

-

Prompt Engineering Tips for Coding:

- **Be Specific:** Clearly define the programming language, framework, libraries, and desired functionality. The more specific your prompt, the more accurate the AI's response.

- **Input-Output Examples:** When possible, provide examples of input data and the expected output to help the AI understand your requirements better.

- **Iterative Refinement:** Don't hesitate to refine your prompts based on the AI's initial responses. Add more details, clarify your requirements, or ask follow-up questions to guide the AI towards the desired solution.

- **Test and Verify:** Always thoroughly test and verify any code generated by AI before using it in a production environment.

Ethical Considerations and Precautions:

- **Code Ownership:** Understand the terms and conditions of the AI code generation tool you're using regarding ownership of the generated code.

- **Security:** Exercise caution when using AI-generated code in critical systems or applications that handle sensitive data. Conduct thorough security reviews and testing.

- **Bias:** Be aware that AI models can sometimes perpetuate biases present in their training data. Scrutinize the generated code for any potential biases and make necessary corrections.

- **Learning Tool:** View AI-generated code as a learning opportunity. Analyze how it's structured, understand the logic behind it, and use it as inspiration for your own coding practices.

By embracing AI as your coding companion and mastering prompt engineering for programming tasks, you can elevate your skills, accelerate your development process, and create more innovative and efficient software solutions.

Chapter 7

Advanced Prompt Engineering Techniques

As you advance in your prompt engineering journey, you'll encounter scenarios that require more than just basic prompts. In this chapter, we'll explore advanced techniques that empower you to guide AI models toward generating the precise and insightful responses you seek. These techniques involve a combination of breaking down complex tasks, incorporating relevant context, and mitigating biases to ensure fair and accurate results.

1. Handling Complex Prompts: The Art of Decomposition

When faced with a complex task, it's tempting to throw the entire problem at an AI model and hope for the best. However, a more strategic approach is to break down the task into smaller, more manageable components. This allows you to guide the model through the process step-by-step, ensuring that each aspect is addressed thoroughly.

Example: Creating a Comprehensive Marketing Campaign

Complex Prompt:

"Develop a comprehensive marketing campaign for a new vegan skincare product, targeting environmentally conscious millennials."

Breakdown:

1. **Target Audience Research:** "Identify the demographics, interests, values, and pain points of environmentally conscious millennials interested in skincare."

2. **Brand Positioning:** "Craft a unique brand identity for the vegan skincare product that resonates with the target audience, emphasizing sustainability and ethical sourcing."

3. **Messaging Strategy:** "Develop key messages and slogans that highlight the product's benefits, eco-friendly attributes, and appeal to the target audience's values."

4. **Content Creation:** "Outline a content calendar for various platforms (social media, blog, email), including engaging visuals, informative articles, and interactive content."

5. **Channel Selection:** "Identify the most effective online and offline channels to reach the target audience, considering budget and potential reach."

6. **Campaign Measurement:** "Establish key performance indicators (KPIs) to track the success of the campaign, such as website traffic, social media engagement, and sales conversions."

By decomposing this complex prompt, you provide a clear roadmap for the AI model, ensuring a well-structured and comprehensive marketing campaign.

2. Incorporating Context Effectively: Guiding Model Understanding

Providing context is akin to giving the AI model a map and compass for your desired destination. It provides the necessary background information, constraints, and examples to ensure the AI model generates responses that align with your expectations and requirements.

Example: Writing a Persuasive Legal Brief

Prompt (Without Context): "Write a legal brief on the topic of self-driving cars."

Prompt (With Context): "You are a lawyer representing a client who was injured in an accident involving a self-driving car. Draft a persuasive legal brief arguing for the client's right to compensation, citing relevant case law and emphasizing the manufacturer's liability for the vehicle's autonomous systems."

By adding context about the legal role, client situation, and specific argument, the AI model can generate a much more focused and effective legal brief.

3. Addressing Bias in AI Responses: Ensuring Fairness and Accuracy

AI models, like any technology, can inherit biases present in their training data. These biases can manifest as stereotypes, discriminatory language, or skewed perspectives. Addressing these biases is crucial for ensuring the fairness and accuracy of AI-generated content.

Example: Creating a Job Description

Prompt (Without Bias Mitigation): "Write a job description for a construction worker."

Prompt (With Bias Mitigation): "Write a job description for a construction worker, avoiding any gender-specific language or assumptions about physical abilities. Focus on the required skills, experience, and qualifications."

By explicitly instructing the model to avoid stereotypes and focus on relevant criteria, you can mitigate the risk of bias in the generated job description.

Examples of Prompt Refinement (Enhanced):

- **Initial Prompt:** "What are the benefits of meditation?"

- **Revised Prompt:** "List five scientifically-proven benefits of mindfulness meditation for reducing stress and improving mental well-being, citing reputable sources."

- **Initial Prompt:** "Write a marketing email about our new product."

- **Revised Prompt:** "Draft a persuasive marketing email for our new [product name], highlighting its unique features, benefits, and a limited-time discount offer. The target audience is health-conscious individuals aged 30-45."

By incorporating these advanced techniques, you can elevate your prompt engineering skills and achieve remarkable results in diverse applications, ensuring that your AI interactions are productive, accurate, and ethically sound.

Absolutely! Let's enhance Chapter 8 with a deeper dive and illustrative examples:

Chapter 8

Evaluating and Improving Prompt Performance

As you hone your prompt engineering skills, the ability to assess and refine your prompts becomes crucial. This chapter delves into the methods and metrics you can employ to gauge the effectiveness of your prompts and iteratively enhance them to achieve your desired outcomes.

Why Evaluate Prompt Performance?

- **Optimizing AI Interactions:** Evaluating prompt performance helps you understand what works and what doesn't. This knowledge allows you to fine-tune your prompts to elicit the most relevant, accurate, and insightful responses from AI models.

  *Example: If a prompt for generating product descriptions yields bland results, evaluation helps you pinpoint the issue – perhaps the prompt lacks specifics about the target audience or desired tone.

- **Identifying Weaknesses:** By analyzing the outputs generated by different prompts, you can identify weaknesses in your approach, such as ambiguous phrasing, lack of context, or unclear instructions. This helps you avoid pitfalls and refine your prompts for better results.

  *Example: If a prompt for summarizing a scientific article generates an overly technical summary, you can revise it to be more concise and understandable for a general audience.

- **Continuous Improvement:** Prompt engineering is an iterative process. Evaluating and improving your prompts over time allows you to learn from your experiences, adapt to the evolving capabilities of AI models, and continually enhance your skills.

  *Example: You might start with a basic prompt for generating code and gradually refine it to include more specific instructions and examples, resulting in more accurate and tailored code snippets.

Key Metrics for Evaluating Prompt Performance:

1. **Relevance:**

   - **Question:** Does the AI model's response directly address the question or task outlined in the prompt?
   - **Example:** If your prompt asks for the capital of France, the relevant response would be "Paris," not a description of French cuisine.

2. **Accuracy:**

   - **Question:** Is the information provided by the AI model factually correct and reliable?
   - **Example:** If your prompt requests information about historical events, the response should align with established historical records and not contain fabricated details.

3. **Coherence:**

- **Question:** Is the AI model's response well-structured, easy to understand, and free from logical inconsistencies?
- **Example:** A coherent response should have a logical flow of ideas, clear transitions between sentences, and avoid contradictory statements.

4. **Creativity (If Applicable):**

- **Question:** For creative tasks like writing poems or generating story ideas, does the response demonstrate originality, imagination, and novelty?
- **Example:** If you ask for a poem about the moon, a creative response might use unique metaphors and imagery instead of relying on clichés.

5. **Efficiency:**

- **Question:** How quickly does the AI model generate a response? Is the response generated within a reasonable timeframe for your needs?
- **Example:** For a real-time chatbot application, efficiency is crucial to maintain a smooth and engaging conversation with users.

Methods for Evaluating Prompt Performance (In-Depth):

1. **Human Evaluation:**

- **Approach:** Engage human evaluators to assess AI responses based on predefined criteria. Use rating scales (e.g., 1-5) for quantitative assessment and gather qualitative feedback.
- **Example:** Ask evaluators to rate the relevance, accuracy, and coherence of AI-generated summaries of news articles, providing specific comments on strengths and weaknesses.

2. **Automated Metrics:**

   - **Approach:** Utilize established metrics like BLEU for machine translation or ROUGE for summarization. Also, explore custom metrics tailored to your specific tasks.
   - **Example:** For a question-answering system, measure the percentage of questions the AI answers correctly and the time it takes to generate responses.

3. **A/B Testing:**

   - **Approach:** Compare the performance of two different prompts on the same task, using a statistically significant sample size.
   - **Example:** Test two different prompts for generating social media captions, and analyze metrics like engagement rate and click-through rate to determine the winner.

4. **Benchmarking:**

   - **Approach:** Compare your prompts and AI-generated responses to established benchmarks or the results of other prompt engineers.
   - **Example:** If you're developing an AI model for medical diagnosis, compare its performance on standardized test cases to those of other state-of-the-art models.

Prompt Refinement Strategies (In-Depth):

1. **Iterative Prompting:** Break down complex tasks into a series of smaller, more manageable prompts, refining each based on the previous response.

- **Example:** Instead of asking for a complete essay, first request an outline, then ask for paragraphs based on the outline, refining the prompt at each step.

2. **Few-Shot Learning:** Provide the AI model with a few examples of desired output before asking it to generate a response.

    - **Example:** Before asking for a movie review, give the AI a few examples of well-written reviews to guide its style and tone.

3. **Prompt Chaining:** Chain together multiple prompts to create a multi-step process.

    - **Example:** First ask the AI to generate a list of potential research topics, then ask for an outline for a specific topic, and finally request a draft of the introduction.

4. **Feedback Loop:** Continuously provide feedback to the AI model on the quality of its responses to help it learn and improve.

    - **Example:** If the AI generates a factually incorrect response, correct it and explain why it was wrong. This feedback can be incorporated into the model's learning process.

By mastering these evaluation methods and refinement strategies, you'll be well-equipped to navigate the iterative process of prompt engineering, consistently improving the effectiveness of your prompts and unlocking the full potential of AI models for your specific needs.

Chapter 9

Addressing Bias and Ethical Considerations in Prompt Engineering

As AI systems become increasingly integrated into our daily lives, it is imperative to address the ethical considerations and potential biases that can arise in prompt engineering. This chapter delves into the challenges of bias, misinformation, and the responsible use of AI to ensure that prompt engineering is employed ethically and for the betterment of society.

Understanding Bias in AI Models: Unmasking the Hidden Influences

AI models, like sponges, absorb information from the data they're trained on. If that data contains biases, the model inadvertently learns and perpetuates those biases in its outputs. This can manifest in several ways:

- **Gender Bias:** An AI model might exhibit gender stereotypes when asked to generate text about certain professions or social roles. For example, it might default to male pronouns when describing doctors or engineers and female pronouns when describing nurses or teachers.
- **Racial Bias:** The model might inadvertently associate certain characteristics or behaviors with specific racial groups, leading to discriminatory or harmful outputs. For instance, it might generate biased responses when asked about crime rates or job suitability.
- **Socioeconomic Bias:** The model might make assumptions about individuals based on their socioeconomic status, leading to unequal treatment or representation in AI-generated content. For example, it might prioritize information about luxury brands when asked for product recommendations.

Unmasking and Mitigating Bias in Prompts: Strategies for Responsible AI

- **Mindful Wording:** Carefully choose your words to avoid perpetuating stereotypes or discriminatory language. Be explicit in your prompts about the need for inclusivity and fairness.

    - **Example:** Instead of "Describe a typical CEO," use "Describe the qualities of a successful CEO, regardless of gender or background."
- **Explicit Instructions:** Direct the AI model to steer clear of biased language or assumptions based on sensitive attributes like gender, race, ethnicity, or socioeconomic status.

    - **Example:** "Write a job description for a software engineer. Avoid using any gendered language or making assumptions about the candidate's age or cultural background."
- **Diverse Training Data:** Advocate for the use of diverse and representative training data to minimize the risk of bias in AI models. A model trained on a narrow dataset may not be able to generate unbiased responses for a wider range of users.

- **Critical Evaluation:** Scrutinize AI-generated responses for any signs of bias. Be prepared to challenge the model if its output is biased or discriminatory. This might involve refining the prompt, providing additional context, or choosing a different model.

The Challenge of Misinformation: Navigating the Sea of Falsehoods

AI models can sometimes generate false or misleading information, either due to gaps in their knowledge or exposure to inaccurate data during training. This poses a significant challenge, as AI-generated misinformation can spread rapidly and have real-world consequences.

- **Fact-Checking:** Always verify information from AI with reliable sources. Don't blindly trust AI-generated content, especially for critical decisions or sensitive topics. Cross-reference the information with reputable sources and consult domain experts when necessary.

- **Transparency:** Be transparent about the use of AI in generating content. Clearly disclose when you have used AI assistance to avoid misleading your audience or misrepresenting your work.

- **Accountability:** Take responsibility for the content you create or share, even if it was generated with the help of AI. Be prepared to correct any inaccuracies or misleading information that may arise from AI-generated content.

Ethical Use of AI in Prompt Engineering: Guiding Principles

- **Beneficial Use:** Strive to use AI prompt engineering for purposes that align with ethical principles and benefit society. Avoid using AI for malicious purposes, such as generating harmful content or manipulating public opinion.

- **Transparency and Explainability:** Be transparent about how you are using AI and, when possible, provide explanations for the AI's decision-making process. This can help build trust with your audience and mitigate the risks of misinformation.

- **Fairness and Non-discrimination:** Ensure that your prompts and the AI-generated content they produce do not discriminate against any individuals or groups based on protected characteristics.

- **Privacy and Security:** Protect the privacy and security of individuals by responsibly handling personal data and avoiding prompts that could lead to the disclosure of sensitive information.

The Role of Prompt Engineers: Shaping the Future of AI

As prompt engineers, you wield significant influence over how AI is used and perceived. By adhering to ethical principles, you can help ensure that AI is a force for good in the world. Your role includes:

- **Promoting Responsible AI Use:** Advocate for the development and deployment of AI systems that are transparent, fair, and accountable.
- **Educating Others:** Help raise awareness about the potential biases and limitations of AI models. Encourage critical thinking and skepticism when consuming AI-generated content.
- **Championing Diversity and Inclusion:** Promote the use of diverse training data and the development of AI models that cater to a wide range of users.
- **Guiding Ethical Development:** Collaborate with AI developers and researchers to ensure that ethical considerations are embedded in the design and development of AI systems.

By embracing these ethical principles and actively working to mitigate biases, you can play a vital role in shaping a future where AI is a tool for good, enhancing human capabilities, and contributing to a more equitable and just society.

Chapter 10

Prompt Engineering in Real-World Applications: Case Studies

Prompt engineering isn't just a theoretical concept—it's a powerful tool that is already transforming industries and revolutionizing how we interact with AI. This chapter delves into real-world case studies that showcase the practical applications of prompt engineering across various domains. By examining these examples, we can gain a deeper understanding of how prompt engineering is being used to solve problems, drive innovation, and create value.

Case Study 1: Content Creation and Marketing

- **Challenge:** A digital marketing agency needs to create engaging and diverse content for a variety of clients, but their small team is struggling to keep up with the demand.

- **Solution:** They implement AI-powered content generation tools and leverage prompt engineering to create a wide range of content formats, including:

  - **Social Media Posts:** Prompts can be used to generate catchy captions, thought-provoking questions, and attention-grabbing headlines for different social media platforms.

  - **Example Prompt:** "Write an engaging Instagram caption for a photo of our new sustainable fashion collection, emphasizing its eco-friendly materials and stylish designs."

- **Blog Articles:** AI models can generate blog post outlines, draft entire articles, or even suggest relevant topics based on current trends.

- **Example Prompt:** "Draft a blog post about the top 10 tips for reducing household waste, including actionable advice and practical examples."

- **Email Marketing Campaigns:** AI can personalize email subject lines, body copy, and calls to action based on customer data and preferences.

- **Example Prompt:** "Write a personalized email to [customer name] recommending products from our new collection based on their previous purchase history."

- **Impact:** By using AI prompt engineering, the marketing agency significantly increases its content production capacity, allowing it to serve more clients and deliver high-quality content that resonates with target audiences.

Case Study 2: Customer Service and Support

- **Challenge:** A large e-commerce company receives thousands of customer inquiries daily, overwhelming its customer support team and leading to long response times.

- **Solution:** The company deploys an AI-powered chatbot that uses prompt engineering to understand customer queries and generate accurate and helpful responses.

- **Prompt:** "Customer is asking how to track their order. Provide them with step-by-step instructions and the estimated delivery date based on their order number."

- **Impact:** The AI chatbot handles a significant portion of customer inquiries, reducing the burden on human agents, improving response times, and increasing customer satisfaction.

Case Study 3: Healthcare and Medical Research

- **Challenge:** A research team is investigating the potential of a new drug for treating a rare disease. They need to analyze vast amounts of scientific literature and clinical trial data to assess the drug's efficacy and safety.

- **Solution:** They employ AI prompt engineering to extract relevant information from research papers, clinical trial reports, and patient records.

  - **Example Prompt:** "Summarize the findings of clinical trials investigating the efficacy of [drug name] in treating [disease name]. Highlight any potential side effects or safety concerns."

- **Impact:** AI-powered prompt engineering accelerates the research process, allowing the team to quickly identify relevant information, synthesize findings, and make informed decisions about the drug's development.

Case Study 4: Software Development and Engineering

- **Challenge:** A software development team is working on a complex project with tight deadlines. They need to streamline their coding process and reduce the risk of errors.

- **Solution:** They integrate AI-powered code generation tools into their workflow. Using prompt engineering, developers can describe the desired functionality in natural language, and the AI model generates corresponding code snippets.

    - **Example Prompt:** "Write a Python function that takes a list of numbers and returns the median value."
- **Impact:** AI-assisted code generation significantly improves developer productivity, allowing them to focus on higher-level tasks, reducing the occurrence of bugs, and accelerating the development process.

Case Study 5: Education and Training

- **Challenge:** A language learning platform wants to personalize the learning experience for its users, catering to their individual needs and learning styles.

- **Solution:** The platform utilizes AI prompt engineering to create adaptive learning paths. By analyzing each user's performance and preferences, the AI model can generate personalized lesson plans, practice exercises, and feedback.

    - **Example Prompt:** "Based on [user's] current proficiency level and interests, generate a customized lesson plan focusing on [language skill] and incorporating [topic of interest]."
- **Impact:** Personalized learning powered by AI significantly improves student engagement and motivation, leading to better learning outcomes and faster

progress.

These case studies illustrate the diverse and impactful applications of prompt engineering in the real world. As AI technology continues to evolve, we can anticipate even more innovative and transformative uses of prompt engineering in the years to come.

Chapter 11

The Future of AI Prompt Engineering: Navigating the Evolving Landscape

As we stand on the precipice of an AI revolution, the future of prompt engineering is brimming with possibilities. In this chapter, we'll explore emerging trends, potential advancements, and the ethical considerations that will shape the evolving landscape of prompt engineering.

Emerging Trends:

1. **Specialized Prompt Engineering:** As AI models become increasingly specialized for specific domains, such as medicine, law, finance, or creative writing, we'll see a rise in specialized prompt engineering techniques tailored to these fields. Prompt engineers will need to develop domain-specific expertise to craft effective prompts that elicit accurate and nuanced responses from these specialized models.

2. **Prompt Engineering as a Service (PEaaS):** The growing demand for high-quality prompts and the increasing complexity of AI models will likely lead to the emergence of Prompt Engineering as a Service (PEaaS). These platforms will offer pre-built prompts, prompt optimization tools, and even professional prompt engineering consulting services, making it easier for businesses and individuals to harness the power of AI.

3. **Community-Driven Prompt Libraries:** Open-source prompt libraries are already gaining traction, allowing prompt engineers to share their expertise, collaborate on projects, and learn from each other. This democratization of prompt engineering knowledge will accelerate innovation and make it easier for

newcomers to get started.

4. **Prompt Engineering for Multimodal Models:** AI models are no longer limited to text; they can now process and generate images, audio, and video. This rise of multimodal models will require prompt engineers to develop new techniques for crafting prompts that incorporate multiple modalities, such as generating images from text descriptions or creating video summaries based on spoken language.

5. **Personalization and Customization:** The future of prompt engineering will likely involve a greater focus on personalization and customization. Prompt engineers will develop tools and techniques that allow users to tailor prompts to their specific needs, preferences, and goals, ensuring that AI-generated content is relevant and meaningful to them.

Potential Advancements:

1. **Automated Prompt Optimization:** Research is underway to develop AI-powered tools that can automatically optimize prompts based on feedback and performance data. These tools will leverage techniques like reinforcement learning to iteratively refine prompts, making them more effective and efficient over time.

2. **Prompt Engineering Frameworks:** As the field matures, we can expect the development of standardized frameworks and best practices for prompt engineering. These frameworks will provide guidance on prompt structure, evaluation metrics, and optimization strategies, making it easier for both experts

and beginners to navigate the complexities of prompt engineering.

3. **Prompt Engineering Education:** With the growing demand for skilled prompt engineers, educational institutions and online learning platforms will likely offer courses and certifications in prompt engineering. This will help to formalize the field and equip learners with the knowledge and skills needed to excel in this emerging discipline.

4. **Explainable AI and Prompt Engineering:** Efforts to make AI models more transparent and explainable will extend to prompt engineering. Researchers are developing techniques to visualize how AI models interpret and respond to prompts, giving users deeper insights into the underlying decision-making process.

Ethical Considerations:

As prompt engineering becomes more powerful, ethical considerations will become increasingly important. We must grapple with issues such as:

- **Bias Amplification:** How can we ensure that prompt engineering doesn't inadvertently amplify existing biases in AI models?
- **Misinformation and Disinformation:** What safeguards can we put in place to prevent the malicious use of prompt engineering to generate and spread false or harmful information?
- **Transparency and Accountability:** How can we ensure transparency in AI-generated content and hold the creators of AI models accountable for the outputs they produce?

- **Accessibility and Equity:** How can we make prompt engineering accessible to everyone, regardless of their technical expertise or background, to ensure that AI benefits all of society?

The Role of Prompt Engineers: Shaping a Responsible AI Future

Prompt engineers will play a pivotal role in shaping the future of AI. They will be responsible for not only crafting effective prompts but also ensuring that AI is used ethically and responsibly. By staying informed about emerging trends, embracing new advancements, and prioritizing ethical considerations, you can be at the forefront of this exciting and dynamic field.

In conclusion, the future of AI prompt engineering is bright, filled with potential for innovation, growth, and positive societal impact. By approaching this field with a sense of responsibility and a commitment to ethical principles, prompt engineers can help ensure that AI technology is harnessed for the benefit of all.

Chapter 12

Building Your Prompt Engineering Toolkit

As you embark on your journey as a prompt engineer, having the right tools at your disposal can significantly enhance your effectiveness and productivity. In this chapter, we'll explore a variety of resources, platforms, and techniques that you can leverage to build a comprehensive prompt engineering toolkit.

Essential Components of Your Toolkit:

1. **Prompt Libraries and Repositories (Enhanced):**
- **Hugging Face Transformers:**

    - **Model Hub:** This extensive collection of pre-trained models includes powerful tools like BERT, GPT-2, and T5, catering to tasks like text classification, translation, summarization, and question-answering. For instance, you can easily find models fine-tuned for sentiment analysis, named entity recognition, or even language generation in specific domains.

    - **Datasets:** Access a vast array of datasets to train and evaluate your own models. These datasets span various domains, from text and audio to images and video, enabling you to create models tailored to your specific needs. For instance, you might find a dataset of medical images to train a model for diagnosis or a dataset of customer reviews for sentiment analysis.

- **Spaces:** Explore interactive demos and applications built with Hugging Face models. These Spaces allow you to test out models in real-time, experiment with different prompts, and gain inspiration for your own projects. For example, you could test a translation model by inputting text in one language and observing the translated output.

- **Community:** Participate in discussions, ask questions, and share your work with a vibrant community of AI enthusiasts and experts. The Hugging Face community is a valuable resource for learning, collaboration, and staying up-to-date with the latest trends in the field.

- **PromptBase:**

  - **Marketplace:** This platform offers a wide array of pre-made prompts for various tasks and AI models. These prompts have often been refined and optimized for specific use cases, saving you time and effort in crafting your own. For example, you might find prompts for generating marketing copy, writing code, or creating artwork.

  - **Prompt Collections:** Explore curated collections of prompts organized by topic or task. These collections can be a valuable source of inspiration and a starting point for your own experiments. For instance, you could browse a collection of prompts for generating creative writing prompts or prompts for summarizing research papers.

- **Prompt Evaluation:** See ratings and reviews of prompts to help you choose the best ones for your needs. This feedback from other users can be invaluable in identifying high-quality and effective prompts.

- **OpenAI Cookbook:**

  - **Example Prompts:** The OpenAI Cookbook is a treasure trove of example prompts for a wide range of tasks and AI models. These examples showcase different prompting techniques and strategies, providing inspiration and guidance for your own prompt engineering efforts.

  - **Best Practices:** Learn from the collective wisdom of OpenAI's experts and community members as they share best practices for crafting effective prompts. These best practices cover aspects like clear instructions, context setting, and iterative refinement.

  - **Tutorials:** Follow step-by-step tutorials on how to use OpenAI models like GPT-3 and ChatGPT for specific tasks. These tutorials provide hands-on guidance and practical tips for getting the most out of these powerful models.

2. Prompt Optimization and Evaluation Tools:

- **PromptLayer:**

  - **Prompt Tracking:** Keep a meticulous record of your prompts, their variations, and the corresponding AI responses. This helps you track your progress, analyze patterns, and identify areas for improvement.

- ○ **Model Comparison:** Test your prompts across different AI models to assess their performance and identify the most suitable model for your task.

- ○ **Performance Metrics:** Monitor key metrics like response quality, relevance, and accuracy to evaluate the effectiveness of your prompts and track their improvement over time.

- **Scale Spellbook:**

  - ○ **Prompt Generation:** Leverage templates and suggestions to quickly generate high-quality prompts. This can be particularly helpful when you're starting or need inspiration for a new task.

  - ○ **Prompt Evaluation:** Get feedback on your prompts from other users and experts. This feedback can provide valuable insights into areas where your prompts can be strengthened or refined.

  - ○ **Prompt Optimization:** Use data-driven insights to iteratively refine your prompts based on performance metrics and user feedback. This helps you create prompts that consistently elicit high-quality responses from AI models.

3. Prompt Engineering Frameworks and Guides:

- **LangChain:**

- **Chain Creation:** Create complex workflows by chaining together multiple prompts and actions. This allows you to break down complex tasks into manageable steps, improving the accuracy and control of AI-generated outputs.

- **Agent Integration:** Integrate language models with other tools and services to build powerful applications. For example, you could create a chatbot that uses a language model to understand user input and then interacts with a database to retrieve relevant information.

- **DeepLearning.AI Prompt Engineering for Developers:**

  - **Comprehensive Course:** This course offers a deep dive into the principles and techniques of prompt engineering, covering everything from basic prompt design to advanced strategies for optimization and evaluation.

  - **Hands-On Projects:** Apply your knowledge through practical projects that challenge you to craft effective prompts for various tasks and AI models. These projects provide valuable hands-on experience and allow you to build a portfolio of prompt engineering work.

  - **Expert Guidance:** Learn from industry experts and experienced practitioners who share their insights and tips for success in the field of prompt engineering.

4. Community Resources and Collaboration Platforms:

- **OpenAI Discord Server:**

  - **Vibrant Community:** Engage with a passionate community of AI enthusiasts, prompt engineers, and OpenAI staff. The server offers a wide range of channels for discussions, questions, and collaboration.

  - **Real-Time Interaction:** Participate in real-time discussions and get immediate feedback on your prompts and ideas.

  - **Networking Opportunities:** Connect with other prompt engineers, learn about their projects, and find potential collaborators.

- **Reddit Communities (r/PromptEngineering and r/MachineLearning):**

  - **Thriving Forums:** These subreddits provide a platform for sharing prompts, discussing techniques, asking questions, and learning from the experiences of others. You can find a wealth of information and support within these communities.

  - **Diverse Perspectives:** Engage with users from different backgrounds and expertise levels, gaining exposure to a wide range of prompt engineering approaches and ideas.

- **Twitter:**

- **Stay Informed:** Follow relevant hashtags like #PromptEngineering, #AI, and #ChatGPT to stay up-to-date on the latest trends, news, and discussions in the field.

- **Connect with Experts:** Follow leading researchers, practitioners, and organizations to gain insights into the latest developments and best practices.

- **Share Your Work:** Showcase your prompt engineering projects and connect with other practitioners to get feedback and build your network.

By leveraging these resources and actively participating in the prompt engineering community, you can accelerate your learning, expand your toolkit, and unlock the full potential of AI to achieve your goals.

Chapter 13

Prompt Engineering for Specific AI Models

While the foundational principles of prompt engineering apply universally, mastering the nuances of specific AI models is key to unlocking their full potential. This chapter delves into tailored strategies and examples for crafting effective prompts for two prominent models: ChatGPT and GPT-4.

ChatGPT: The Conversational Maestro

Renowned for its conversational prowess, ChatGPT thrives in scenarios that demand natural language interaction, creative text generation, and informative responses. Here's how to harness its strengths:

Prompting Strategies:

- **System-Level Instructions:** Guide ChatGPT's overall behavior and tone by providing initial instructions.

    - **Example:** "You are a friendly and helpful AI assistant specializing in travel recommendations." This sets the context for subsequent interactions.

-

- **Clear and Concise Prompts:** Maintain clarity and conciseness in your prompts to avoid ambiguity and ensure ChatGPT understands your intent.

    - **Example:** Instead of "Tell me about Paris," ask "What are the top 5 must-see attractions in Paris for first-time visitors?"

- **Open-Ended vs. Specific Prompts:** Use open-ended prompts to encourage creativity and specific prompts for factual information.

  - **Open-Ended Example:** "Imagine you're a time traveler. Describe your experience visiting ancient Rome."
  - **Specific Example:** "List the major causes and consequences of the Industrial Revolution."
- **Iterative Refinement:** Engage in a conversation with ChatGPT, refining your prompts based on its responses. Ask follow-up questions or provide additional context to guide it towards more accurate or detailed answers.

  - **Example:** If ChatGPT provides a generic answer, ask "Can you provide more specific examples of how AI is being used in healthcare?"

Example Prompts for ChatGPT:

- **Creative Writing:** "Write a short story about a group of friends who discover a hidden portal to another dimension."

- **Information Retrieval:** "What are the health benefits of a Mediterranean diet, and how can I incorporate it into my daily meals?"

- **Brainstorming:** "Help me brainstorm ideas for a fundraising event for our local animal shelter."

- **Translation:** "Translate this paragraph from English to French, ensuring the translation is accurate and captures the original tone."

GPT-4: The Advanced Reasoning Powerhouse

Building upon the strengths of ChatGPT, GPT-4 showcases enhanced capabilities in reasoning, problem-solving, and handling complex prompts. Let's explore strategies to maximize its potential:

Prompting Strategies:

- **Utilize Advanced Reasoning:** Leverage GPT-4's ability to analyze, synthesize, and draw conclusions.

    - **Example:** "Given these economic indicators [insert data], predict the likely impact of a rise in interest rates on the housing market."

- **Experiment with Prompt Formats:** GPT-4 can handle diverse formats like bullet points, tables, and code snippets. Experiment to find the most effective format for your task.

    - **Example:** "Create a table comparing the features and pricing of the top 5 smartphones in the market."

- **Provide Detailed Instructions and Examples:** Be explicit about the desired format, content, and style of the output. Use examples to illustrate your expectations.

    - **Example:** "Write a Python function to calculate the average of a list of numbers. The function should handle empty lists and return None in such cases."

- **Chain Prompts for Complex Tasks:** Break down complex tasks into smaller, sequential prompts to guide GPT-4 through a step-by-step process.

  - **Example:**
    1. "Generate a list of potential research topics related to climate change."
    2. "Select one topic from the list and create a detailed research outline."
    3. "Write an introduction for a research paper on the chosen topic."

Example Prompts for GPT-4:

- **Code Generation:** "Write a Python script to scrape product data from an e-commerce website."

- **Complex Analysis:** "Analyze the geopolitical factors that contributed to the outbreak of World War II."

- **Creative Problem Solving:** "Devise a strategy for a company to reduce its carbon footprint while maintaining profitability."

By understanding the unique strengths and capabilities of ChatGPT and GPT-4, you can tailor your prompts to elicit the most relevant, accurate, and insightful responses, empowering you to achieve your goals efficiently and effectively. Remember, continuous experimentation and refinement of your prompts are key to unlocking the full potential of these powerful AI models.

Chapter 14

Common Pitfalls in Prompt Engineering and How to Avoid Them

Prompt engineering, while incredibly powerful, is not without its challenges. Even experienced practitioners can fall prey to common pitfalls that can hinder the effectiveness of their prompts and lead to suboptimal results. In this chapter, we'll shine a light on these pitfalls, analyze their consequences, and equip you with practical strategies to steer clear of them, ensuring your AI interactions are smooth, productive, and aligned with your goals.

Pitfall 1: Ambiguity and Vagueness

One of the most prevalent mistakes in prompt engineering is crafting prompts that are too broad, ambiguous, or lacking in specificity. This can confuse AI models and lead to responses that are irrelevant, inaccurate, or fail to address the core of your query.

Example:

- **Vague Prompt:** "Tell me about climate change."
- **Consequences:** The AI could provide a general overview, a history, current impacts, or future predictions. The response might be overwhelming or not address your specific interest.
- **Improved Prompt:** "Summarize the key findings of the latest IPCC report on the impact of climate change on global agriculture."

Solution:

Be explicit and precise in your prompts. Clearly state the desired task, format, and level of detail you expect in the AI's response. Use specific keywords and phrases that accurately convey your intent.

Pitfall 2: Insufficient Context

AI models, while intelligent, lack the worldly experience and common sense that humans possess. Failing to provide sufficient context can lead to misinterpretations, factual errors, or responses that miss the mark entirely.

Example:

- **Prompt (Lacking Context):** "What are the benefits?"
- **Consequences:** The AI has no reference point and could list benefits of anything (exercise, a product, a policy). The response will likely be irrelevant to your query.
- **Improved Prompt:** "What are the potential benefits of implementing a four-day workweek for employee well-being and productivity?"

Solution:

Always provide enough context for the AI model to grasp the full picture. This can include background information, references to previous interactions, or specific details about the topic at hand.

Pitfall 3: Overly Complex or Convoluted Prompts

While AI models are becoming increasingly capable of handling complex language, bombarding them with overly long, convoluted, or excessively technical prompts can lead to confusion and errors.

Example:

- **Overly Complex Prompt:** "Analyze the multifaceted socio-economic and geopolitical ramifications of the burgeoning field of artificial intelligence on the global landscape, taking into account the ethical implications and potential for both utopian and dystopian outcomes."

- **Consequences:** The AI might struggle to parse the complex sentence structure and multiple clauses, leading to a response that is either incomplete or misses the core focus of the query.

- **Improved Prompt:** "Analyze the potential impact of artificial intelligence on the global economy and society, considering both positive and negative consequences."

Solution:

Keep your prompts concise and focused. Break down complex ideas into smaller, more digestible chunks. Use clear and direct language, avoiding unnecessary jargon or technical terms.

Pitfall 4: Neglecting to Iterate and Refine

Prompt engineering is an iterative process. Expecting perfect results from the first attempt is unrealistic.

Example:

- **Initial Prompt:** "Write a poem about love." (Too broad)
- **Refined Prompt:** "Write a sonnet about the unrequited love of a young artist for their muse." (More specific and focused)

Solution:

Embrace experimentation and be prepared to refine your prompts based on the AI's responses. Analyze the output, identify areas for improvement, and iterate until you achieve the desired outcome.

Pitfall 5: Overreliance on AI:

AI models are powerful tools, but they are not infallible. Relying solely on AI-generated content without critical evaluation can lead to the spread of misinformation or perpetuate biases.

Example:

- **Overreliance:** Blindly trusting an AI-generated medical diagnosis without consulting a healthcare professional could be dangerous.

Solution:

Always verify the accuracy and reliability of AI-generated content. Use AI as a tool to augment your own knowledge and expertise, not replace it.

Pitfall 6: Ignoring Ethical Considerations:

Prompt engineering raises important ethical concerns, such as bias, misinformation, and potential misuse. Failing to address these concerns can lead to harmful consequences.

Example:

- **Ignoring Bias:** Using a prompt that perpetuates stereotypes or discriminatory language can lead to harmful outputs that reinforce harmful biases.

Solution:

Be mindful of the ethical implications of your prompts and the AI-generated content they produce. Strive to use AI in a responsible and equitable manner, ensuring transparency, fairness, and accountability.

By recognizing and avoiding these common pitfalls, you can become a more effective and responsible prompt engineer, maximizing the benefits of AI while minimizing its potential drawbacks.

Chapter 15

Conclusion and Next Steps: Your Journey as a Prompt Engineer Continues

As we reach the culmination of our exploration into the dynamic realm of AI prompt engineering, it's time to reflect on the knowledge you've acquired, celebrate your accomplishments, and embark on the next phase of your journey in this transformative field.

Recap of Key Learnings:

Throughout this book, we've embarked on a comprehensive journey through the landscape of AI prompt engineering. We've covered a vast spectrum of topics, from the fundamental building blocks of prompts and AI models to advanced techniques and ethical considerations. Let's revisit the key takeaways:

1. **The Foundations:**

- **Understanding AI Models:** We demystified the inner workings of AI models, particularly large language models (LLMs), exploring their transformer architecture, attention mechanisms, and probabilistic nature. We learned how these models process information and generate responses, enabling us to craft more effective prompts.

- **Prompt Anatomy:** We dissected the anatomy of a well-crafted prompt, emphasizing the importance of clarity, specificity, context, instructions, and constraints. We learned how to tailor prompts to different tasks and AI models to achieve desired outcomes.

2. **Prompt Engineering Techniques:**

- **Basic to Advanced:** We progressed from basic prompt engineering techniques, such as using clear language and providing context, to more advanced strategies like prompt decomposition, few-shot learning, and prompt chaining.

- **Real-World Applications:** We explored the practical applications of prompt engineering in diverse fields, including content creation, customer service, healthcare, software development, and education. We saw how prompt engineering is revolutionizing these industries by enhancing productivity, creativity, and innovation.

3. **Ethical Considerations:**

- **Bias Mitigation:** We confronted the challenges of bias in AI models and learned strategies to mitigate them through mindful wording, explicit instructions, diverse training data, and critical evaluation of AI-generated outputs.

- **Misinformation Management:** We emphasized the importance of fact-checking, transparency, and accountability when working with AI-generated content to combat the spread of misinformation.

- **Responsible AI Use:** We discussed the ethical principles that should guide prompt engineering, such as ensuring beneficial use, fairness, non-discrimination, privacy, and security.

Empowering Your Potential: Your Journey as a Prompt Engineer

The knowledge and skills you've gained from this book are just the beginning. The field of prompt engineering is still in its early stages, and there are countless opportunities for exploration, innovation, and impact. Here's how you can continue your journey:

1. **Practice and Experimentation:** The more you practice crafting prompts, the more proficient you'll become. Experiment with different AI models, tasks, and prompt variations. Embrace a spirit of curiosity and don't be afraid to try new things.

2. **Community Engagement:** Join online communities, forums, and social media groups dedicated to prompt engineering. Share your knowledge, learn from others, and collaborate on projects.

3. **Continuous Learning:** Stay informed about the latest advancements in AI and prompt engineering. Read research papers, blogs, and articles. Attend conferences and workshops. Explore new tools and techniques. The field is constantly evolving, and continuous learning is key to staying at the forefront.

4. **Building Projects:** Apply your prompt engineering skills to real-world projects. Whether you're developing AI applications, generating creative content, or solving complex problems, hands-on experience is invaluable for solidifying your knowledge and expanding your skillset.

5. **Sharing Your Knowledge:** Become a mentor and share your expertise with others. Write blog posts, create tutorials, or give presentations on prompt engineering. By teaching others, you'll not only reinforce your own understanding

but also contribute to the growth of the community.

Examples of Next Steps:

- **Specialize in a Domain:** Choose a field that interests you, such as healthcare, law, or finance, and become an expert in prompt engineering for AI models specialized in that domain.
- **Develop Prompt Engineering Tools:** Create your own tools or platforms to streamline the prompt engineering process, such as prompt generators, evaluation frameworks, or optimization algorithms.
- **Research New Techniques:** Explore emerging research areas in prompt engineering, such as few-shot learning, reinforcement learning from human feedback, or the development of explainable AI models.

Conclusion:

Prompt engineering is a powerful skill that can unlock the full potential of AI. As you embark on the next phase of your journey, remember that your role as a prompt engineer is not just about technical expertise, but also about ethical responsibility. By using AI for good, championing fairness and transparency, and promoting responsible AI use, you can help shape a future where AI benefits all of humanity. The future of AI is in your hands – let your creativity and passion guide you as you continue to explore the exciting possibilities of prompt engineering.

AI Prompt Engineering: A Comprehensive Guide

Introduction

This book has taken you on a journey through the exciting and rapidly evolving field of AI prompt engineering. We've delved into the inner workings of AI models, explored various techniques for crafting effective prompts, and examined real-world applications across industries. We've also addressed the ethical considerations and future trends that will shape the development of this powerful tool.

Understanding AI Models

The foundation of prompt engineering lies in understanding how AI models work. We explored the different types of models commonly used in this field, such as Large Language Models (LLMs) like GPT-3 and GPT-4, text-to-image models like DALL-E and Stable Diffusion, and code generation models like Codex and GitHub Copilot.

We delved into the architecture of these models, focusing on transformers and their attention mechanisms, which enable AI to process and understand language in a way that mimics human comprehension. We also discussed the limitations of AI models, such as their potential for bias and their susceptibility to generating incorrect or nonsensical information.

Crafting Effective Prompts: The Essentials

Crafting effective prompts is both an art and a science. We covered the essential elements of a good prompt, including clarity, specificity, context, instructions, and constraints. We learned how to tailor prompts for different tasks and AI models, using clear language, specific keywords, and relevant examples.

We explored different types of prompts, such as instruction-based prompts, question-based prompts, and completion-based prompts. We also discussed the importance of context in prompt engineering, emphasizing how providing background information and relevant details can significantly improve the quality of AI-generated responses.

Prompt Engineering for Writing and Content Creation

Prompt engineering has revolutionized the way we write and create content. We explored how AI can be used as a creative partner, brainstorming ideas, generating outlines, drafting content, and even helping overcome writer's block. We looked at examples of prompts for various writing tasks, from blog posts and articles to poetry and short stories.

Prompt Engineering for Research and Information Gathering

AI is not just a tool for creativity; it's also a powerful research assistant. We explored how prompt engineering can help us find relevant sources, extract key information, summarize complex texts, compare and contrast different perspectives, and even generate reports and presentations.

Prompt Engineering for Code Generation and Programming

AI is transforming the way we code. We delved into how prompt engineering can be used to generate code snippets, refactor existing code, debug errors, and explain complex concepts. We discussed the benefits of AI-assisted coding, such as increased productivity and reduced error rates.

Advanced Prompt Engineering Techniques

As we progressed, we explored more advanced prompt engineering techniques. We learned how to handle complex prompts by breaking them down into smaller, more manageable components. We also discussed the importance of incorporating context effectively and mitigating biases in AI responses.

Evaluating and Improving Prompt Performance

To get the most out of AI, it's crucial to evaluate and refine your prompts. We explored various metrics for evaluating prompt performance, such as relevance, accuracy, coherence, creativity, and efficiency. We also discussed different evaluation methods, including human evaluation, automated metrics, A/B testing, and benchmarking.

Ethical Considerations in Prompt Engineering

The rise of AI raises important ethical considerations. We explored the potential for bias in AI models and how prompt engineering can inadvertently amplify those biases. We discussed the challenge of misinformation and the importance of fact-checking and transparency when using AI-generated content.

We emphasized the need for responsible AI use, adhering to principles of fairness, non-discrimination, privacy, and security. We also highlighted the role of prompt engineers in shaping the future of AI and ensuring that it is used for the benefit of humanity.

The Future of AI Prompt Engineering

The field of prompt engineering is rapidly evolving. We looked ahead to emerging trends, such as specialized prompt engineering, prompt engineering as a service, community-driven prompt libraries, and prompt engineering for multimodal models. We also discussed potential advancements in automated prompt optimization, prompt engineering frameworks, and education.

Building Your Prompt Engineering Toolkit

Finally, we explored the tools and resources that can help you become a proficient prompt engineer. We looked at prompt libraries and repositories, prompt optimization and evaluation tools, prompt engineering frameworks and guides, and community resources and collaboration platforms.

Conclusion: Your Journey Continues

The journey of a prompt engineer is one of continuous learning and exploration. As AI technology continues to advance, new possibilities and challenges will emerge. By staying informed, experimenting, collaborating, and adhering to ethical principles, you can make a significant impact in this exciting and dynamic field. The future of AI is in your hands.

A Final Words : Your Adventure Begins

As you close this book, you've unlocked the door to a world where human ingenuity and artificial intelligence intertwine. Prompt engineering is not just a skill—it's a mindset, a way of thinking that allows you to communicate, collaborate, and create with AI in unprecedented ways.

The journey doesn't end here. The AI landscape is ever-evolving, and as a prompt engineer, you have a front-row seat to witness and participate in its transformation. Stay curious, experiment fearlessly, and embrace the challenges that come your way. The possibilities are boundless.

Remember, prompt engineering isn't just about technical proficiency; it's about wielding this powerful tool responsibly and ethically. Strive to use AI for good, to amplify human creativity, to solve pressing problems, and to create a future that benefits all of humanity.

As you embark on your own adventures in prompt engineering, may this book serve as a compass, guiding you through the uncharted territories of AI.

The future is yours to shape. Now go forth, craft prompts that inspire, inform, and transform, and let your journey as a prompt engineer be filled with discovery, innovation, and impact.

Happy prompting!